This book belongs

Draw a picture
of yourself.

COLOUR US IN!

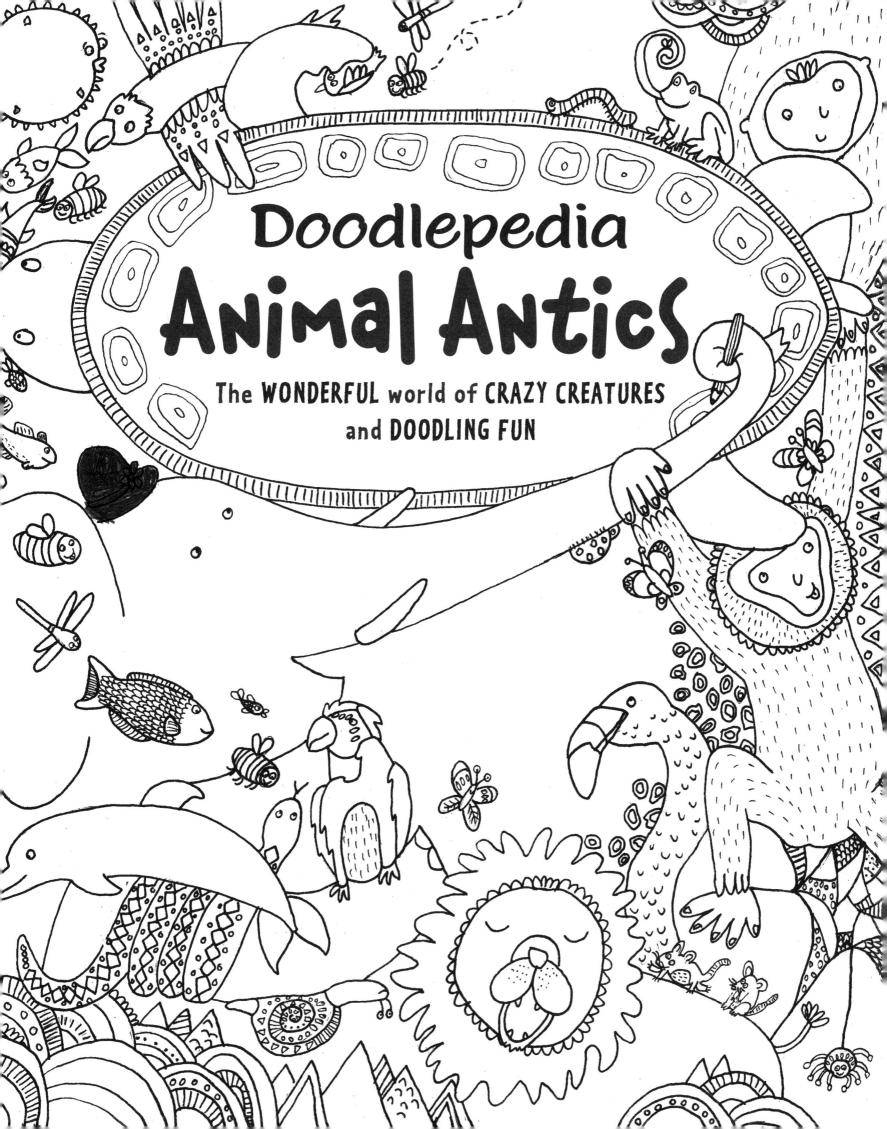

DK

LONDON, NEW YORK, MELBOURNE, MUNICH, AND DELHI

Edited by Laura Palosuo, Lorrie Mack
Designed by Jess Bentall
Text by Laura Palosuo
Fact checker Kim Bryan
Illustrators Emma Atkinson, Holly Blackman, Amber Cassidy, Helen Dodsworth, Carly Epworth, Evan Nave, Jake McDonald, Peter Todd, Dan Woodger, Jay Wright
Design Assistant Charlotte Bull
Managing Editor Penny Smith
Managing Art Editor Marianne Markham
Art director Jane Bull
Category publisher Mary Ling
Producer, Pre-Production Andy Hilliard
Senior Producer Seyhan Esen
Creative Technical Support Sonia Charbonnier

First published in Great Britain in 2013 by
Dorling Kindersley Limited,
80 Strand, London, WC2R 0RL

Copyright© 2013 Dorling Kindersley Limited
A Penguin Company
10 9 8 7 6 5 4 3 2 1
187177 – 02/13

A CIP catalogue record for this book is available from the British Library
ISBN: 978-1-4093-6475-7
Printed and bound in China by Leo Paper Products Ltd.

Discover more at www.dk.com

DRAW MORE STICKY-FOOTED GECKOS CLIMBING OVER THE SLIPPERY WINDOW

COLOUR THE CUNNING CUCKOO'S EGGS TO MATCH THE OTHERS IN THE NEST

Doodlepedia
Animal Antics

The WONDERFUL world of CRAZY CREATURES and DOODLING FUN

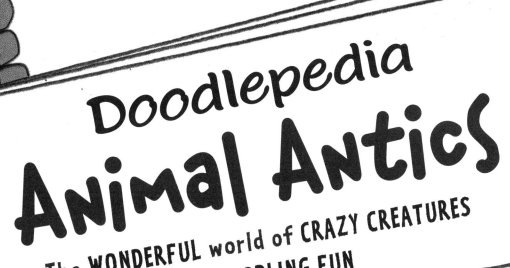

DISCOVER HOW SPIDERS BREATHE UNDER WATER **LEARN** HOW FAR FROGS CAN JUMP

GO **DOODLING** CRAZY IN THE EMPTY BOX

Doodlepedia

Doodlepedia is exactly what it says – a book of doodling! **COLOUR, DESIGN,** and **DRAW** all over the pages and learn as you create. Find out about birds, beavers, bears, bees, butterflies, and lots more! Are you ready for oodles of doodling fun? Then turn the page and begin!

DISCOVER how parrotfish make sand.

COLOUR the beautifully patterned parrotfish.

Pretty polly

Parrotfish have an important job – they keep reefs healthy by scraping away material that builds up on the surface of the coral. However, in doing this, they sometimes break off small pieces of coral. These pass through the gut of the fish and out the other end as white coral sand.

COLOUR IN THE MARKINGS ON THE FISH.

Parrotfish get their name from their tropical colouring as well as their teeth, which are joined together and look a bit like the beak of a parrot.

Parrotfish create much of the white sand on the shores of coral islands.

DRAW PATTERNS ON THE PARROTFISH.

High in the sky!

The sky is full of living creatures. Many birds fly, and some travel long distances from country to country every year. Insects such as butterflies and some beetles fly. In fact, there are billions of insects in the air at any one time. Bats fly. They are the only furry animal that do!

Although penguins are birds, they can't fly – unless you give them a jet pack!

FIND THE ANIMAL THAT SHOULDN'T BE IN THE AIR. THEN COLOUR ALL THE CREATURES THAT REALLY FLY.

FIND the animal that can't really fly.

DRAW MORE PENGUINS PLAYING AND SLIDING ON THE SLOPES.

SOUTH POLE

Penguin playtime

Careful, it's slippery! Penguins are excellent swimmers and spend most of their time in the water. Although they can walk on their flippers, on slippery snow and ice it's quicker for penguins to slide down hills on their belly. Wouldn't you rather toboggan, too?

Adélie Penguins are mostly black with a white front.

Chinstrap Penguins look like they are wearing a black hat!

Emperor Penguins are the biggest of all penguins.

COLOUR IN THE DIFFERENT KINDS OF PENGUIN.

Penguin mums and dads raise their chicks together.

Cheeky Chipmunks

Chipmunks sleep underground through the cold winter months. But instead of living off stored body fat like many other animals, they gather food in their burrows. They then sleep nearby in their nest, waking every few days to have a snack to keep themselves going.

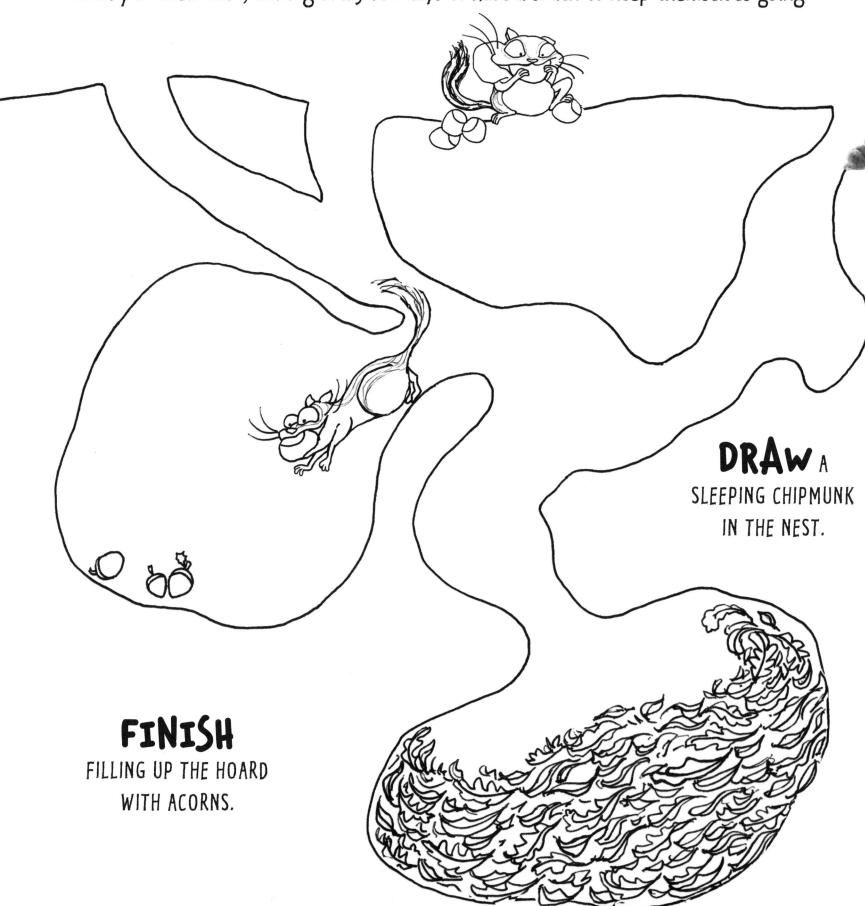

DRAW A SLEEPING CHIPMUNK IN THE NEST.

FINISH FILLING UP THE HOARD WITH ACORNS.

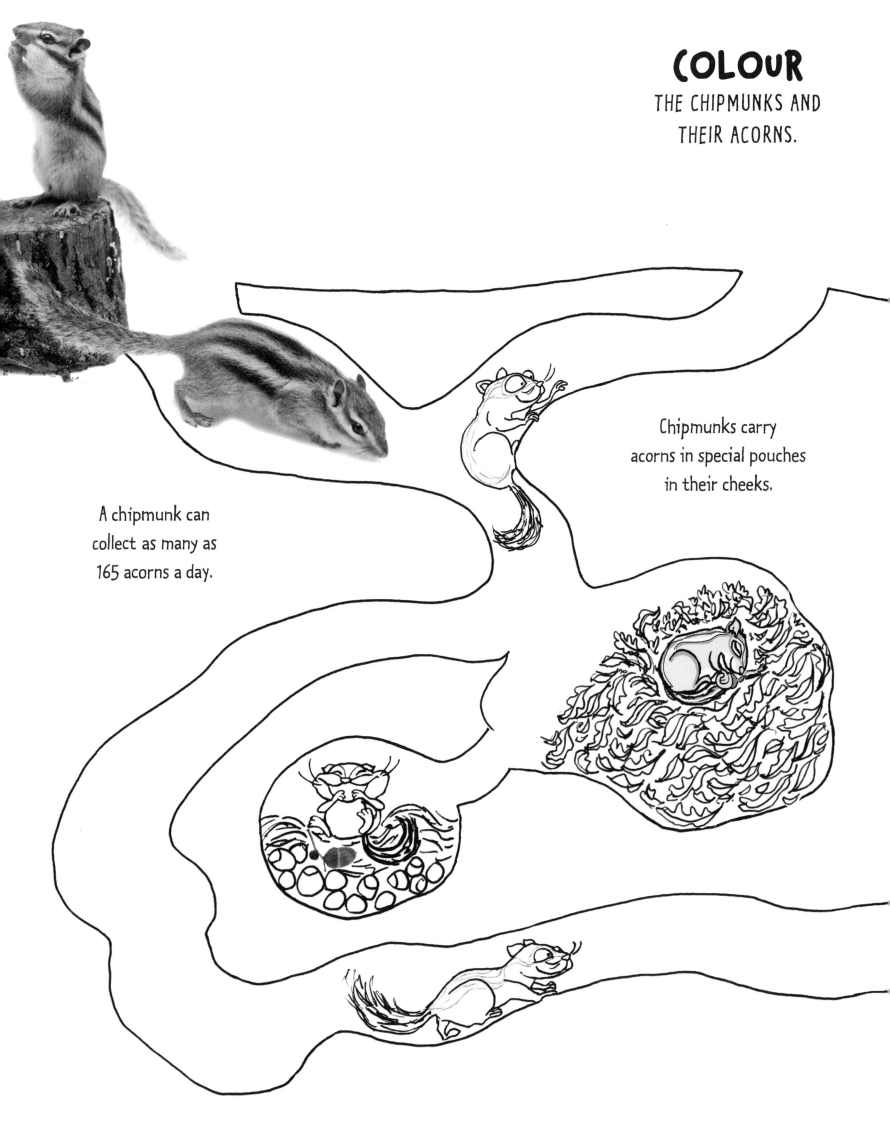

COLOUR
THE CHIPMUNKS AND
THEIR ACORNS.

Chipmunks carry
acorns in special pouches
in their cheeks.

A chipmunk can
collect as many as
165 acorns a day.

Pretty polly

Parrotfish have an important job – they keep reefs healthy by scraping away material that builds up on the surface of the coral. However, in doing this, they sometimes break off small pieces of coral. These pass through the gut of the fish and out the other end as white coral sand.

DRAW PATTERNS ON THE PARROTFISH.

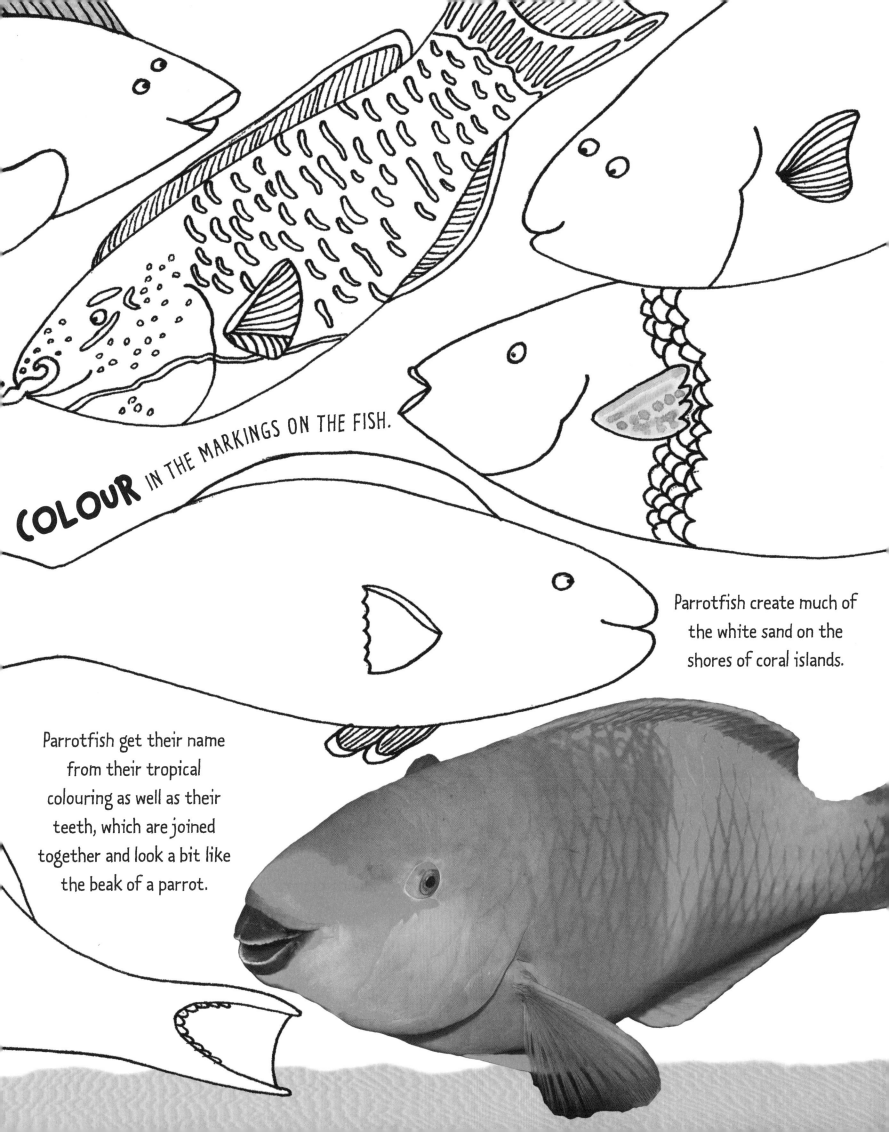

COLOUR IN THE MARKINGS ON THE FISH.

Parrotfish create much of the white sand on the shores of coral islands.

Parrotfish get their name from their tropical colouring as well as their teeth, which are joined together and look a bit like the beak of a parrot.

Ear, Ear!

Elephants are the biggest land animals. They can weigh up to 10 tonnes, or as much as 10 cars! There are three species (types) of elephant: African savanna elephants and African forest elephants live in Africa and Indian elephants live in Asia. One way to tell them apart is by their ears — African elephants have bigger ones.

AFRICA

Look at this African elephant's ears — they're shaped a bit like Africa! On hot days he flaps them to create a cooling breeze.

Indian elephants have smaller ears that are shaped a bit like India.

INDIA

DRAW THE EARS ON THE ELEPHANTS TO SHOW WHETHER THEY'RE AFRICAN OR INDIAN.

Spider webs

Spiders make their webs everywhere – in trees, bushes, and even in people's homes. Spiders use their web to catch insects. Insects either get tangled in the web, or they trip over the threads. This tells the spider to run out and catch the insect. Spiders spin the silk that the web is made from. It comes out of openings called spinnerets near their bottom!

Tangle webs can look a bit messy!

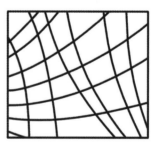

Spiral orb webs are round in shape.

Funnel webs form a tube-like tunnel.

Sheet webs can cover large areas.

DRAW MORE SPIDERS SPINNING WEBS.

Dolphin School

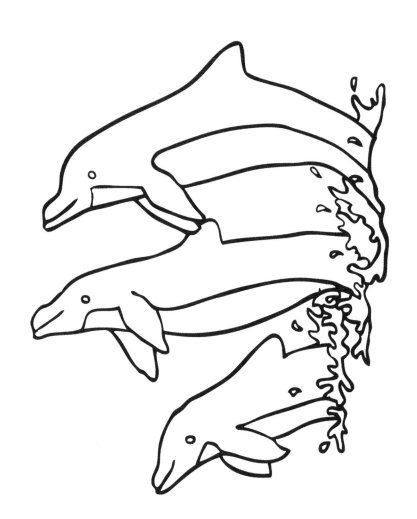

Although dolphins in marine-life centres often perform amazing tricks like swimming on their tail, dolphins in the wild rarely do. That is, unless someone teaches them to. When a bottlenose dolphin was released into the wild off the coast of Australia, scientists were surprised to discover many other dolphins soon performing the same tricks it had learned in captivity. The dolphin had taught its friends!

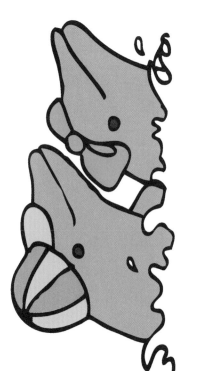

Dolphins are considered to be one of the world's most intelligent animals.

DRAW MORE DOLPHINS PERFORMING THE TRICKS THEY'VE LEARNED.

Bottlenose dolphins get their name from their short, bottle-like beak.

Bowerbird's love nest

To impress a lady, give her... a bit of blue string? It might seem strange to us, but some bowerbird males attract females by building a bower (shelter) and decorating it with blue objects that they've found. And the ladies just love it!

Bowerbirds decorate their bower with man-made objects like bits of plastic and metal, as well as natural ones such as flowers and feathers.

FEMALE

DRAW AND COLOUR

MORE BLUE OBJECTS TO HELP THIS MALE ATTRACT A MATE.

Bowerbirds build their U-shaped bower out of sticks.

MALE

Brown bears' feast

Brown bears love salmon, and have found a clever way to go fishing. They just stand in a river, wait for fish to swim by, and then grab them in their teeth or paws. Sometimes they even catch salmon leaping out of the water!

Brown bears sleep through the winter, so in autumn, they need to eat lots and lots of food to keep them going for all that time.

DRAW MORE SALMON JUMPING OUT OF THE RIVER.

BEWARE OF THE BEARS

Bears sometimes dive in to catch
fish swimming under water.

DRAW MORE CAPUCHIN MONKEYS BREAKING OPEN FRUIT.

The stone "hammers" used by the capuchins can weigh up to 1.7kg (3.7lbs) – that's half the monkey's weight!

Young capuchin monkeys learn to break open fruit by watching older monkeys do it. Monkey see, monkey do.

Monkey business

Capuchin monkeys are very clever and know how to break into the hardest fruit. If the fruit is too hard to open using their hands and teeth, they use tools! First they find somewhere to place the fruit so that it will not move. Then they strike it with a stone to split it open. Dinner is served!

DRAW MORE GECKOS CLIMBING UP AND DOWN THE WINDOW.

Gluey geckos

Do geckos have superpowers? It's easy to think they do as they can walk up almost any surface, including walls and windows. In fact, their superpower is their specialized feet. The bottoms of their toes are covered in tiny hair-like bumps that can cling to the smallest ridge, allowing the gecko to hang on.

The tiny bumps on a gecko's toes allow it to climb up walls and windows.

Geckos eat insects, hunting them in places most other animals can't reach.

Living on land

Land creatures come in all shapes and sizes. This is no surprise because the area of land they come from can be very different. Imagine living in a tropical rainforest, on a high mountain, in the frozen Arctic, or in a hot, dry desert. There's one thing all the animals have in common – each animal is perfectly suited to the place where it lives.

FIND
THE CREATURE
THAT SHOULDN'T
BE ON LAND.

COLOUR
ALL THE DIFFERENT
LAND ANIMALS.

Dressed crab

When they need to hide from predators, dresser crabs know just where to go – to the dressing-up box! Dresser crabs can blend in with their surroundings by attaching nearby objects to their body. They can do this because they have areas on their shell that stick a bit like Velcro.

DRAW MORE OBJECTS FOR THE DRESSER CRAB TO CHOOSE ITS OUTFIT FROM.

Dresser crabs have been known to wear bits of seaweed, coral, and even sea anemones. How fabulous!

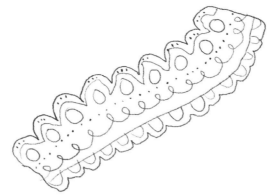

DRAW WHAT THE DRESSER CRAB IS WEARING TO HIDE ITSELF.

If you get sprayed by a skunk, the smell can stay on you for several days.

DRAW MORE SKUNKS SPRAYING.

You've been Skunked!

Eurgh, what's that smell? It's worse than rotten eggs – it's a skunk! When skunks are frightened, they defend themselves by spraying strong, horrible scent from a gland under their tail. Before they spray, skunks give a warning. They stamp their feet and lift up their tail. Some skunks even do a handstand. You've been warned!

Skunks have very good aim. They can can hit a target up to 15m (50ft) away.

Fly fishers

How does a fish hunt for food? With a water pistol, of course! The amazing archerfish catches insects from plants that overhang the water. It knocks them off with a jet of water produced by pressing its tongue against the roof of its mouth and quickly closing the gill covers. It can hit its target from a distance of about 1.5m (5ft)!

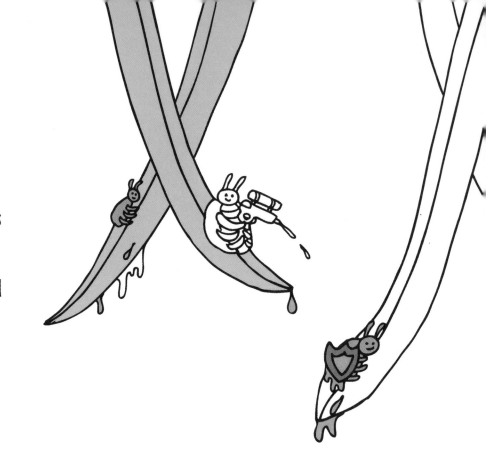

DRAW THE WATER SQUIRTS FROM THE FISH TO THE INSECTS.

Archerfish live in streams and lakes in South East Asia and northen Australia.

ADD BANDS TO THE FISH AND FINISH COLOURING THE PICTURE.

Dancing lemurs

If you ever go down to Madagasgar, you might see lemurs dancing! Most lemurs live in the trees, and leap from branch to branch. If the trees are too far apart the lemurs come down and cross the ground with a sideways jump-hop. At the same time, they hold their arms held out to the sides so it looks like they're dancing!

Madagascar is an island off the coast of Africa. On our globe, it's coloured in red.

DRAW MORE LEMURS DANCING ON THE GROUND.

Can you guess why this is called a
ring-tailed lemur?

Dung beetle race

All dung beetles deserve a medal. They help keep the planet clean by eating dung (animal poo). Dung beetles known as "rollers" make balls out of the dung. They roll the balls to a place where they can be buried to eat later or used to lay their eggs in. Rollers need to roll their balls quickly, or they might be stolen by other dung beetles!

Dung beetles called "dwellers" live in a pile of dung.

DRAW MORE DUNG BEETLES IN THE RACE.

Dung beetles can roll a ball that is up to 10 times their own weight.

"Tunneller" beetles dig a tunnel under the dung to bury it where they find it.

Stick it out!

Giraffes are very good at reaching leaves high up. First, they can grow to be up to 5.5m (18ft) tall – as tall as a two-storey building! Second, their very long tongue gives them extra reach. It can extend to up to 45cm (18in), or the length of 3 bananas!

Giraffes prefer to eat acacia leaves. They use their tongue and teeth to strip them from branches.

DRAW MORE GIRAFFES AND THEIR LONG TONGUES.

Each giraffe has a
distinct pattern of patches
– like a fingerprint!

A giraffe's tongue
is this long!

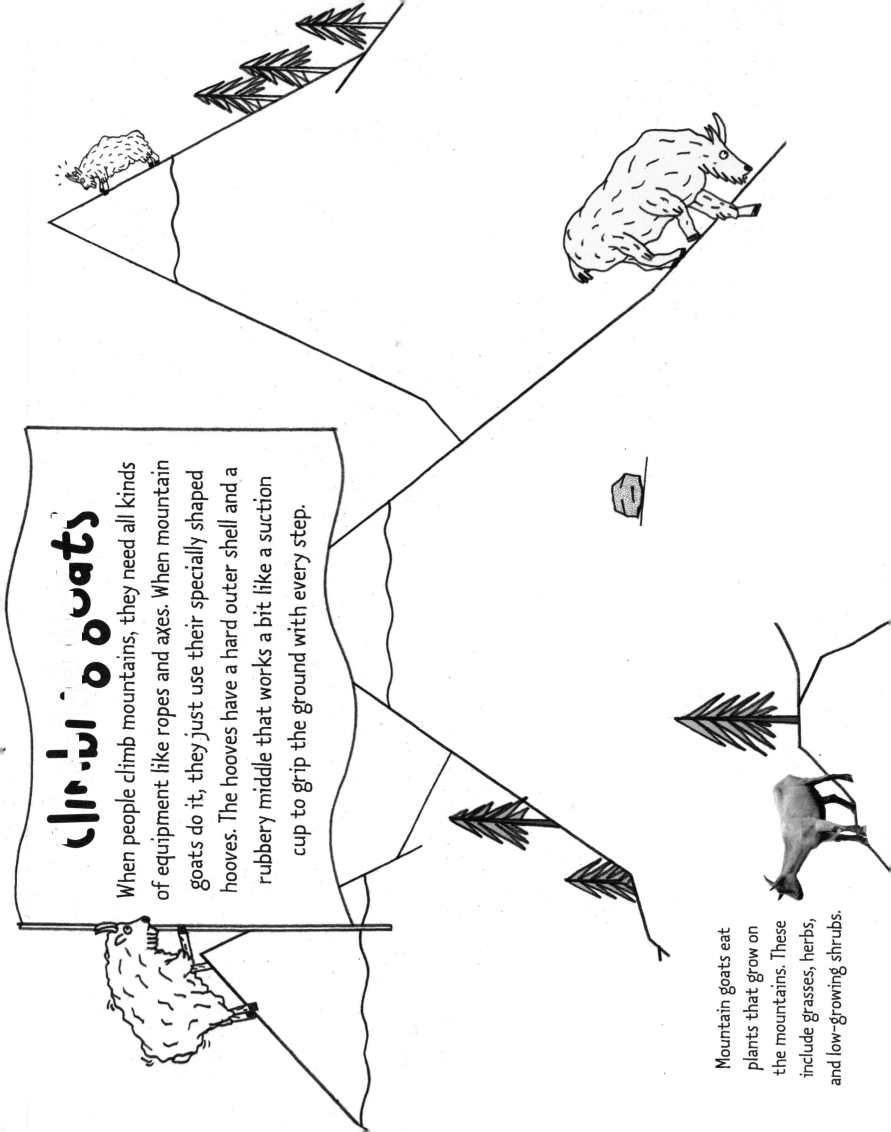

Mountain Goats

When people climb mountains, they need all kinds of equipment like ropes and axes. When mountain goats do it, they just use their specially shaped hooves. The hooves have a hard outer shell and a rubbery middle that works a bit like a suction cup to grip the ground with every step.

Mountain goats eat plants that grow on the mountains. These include grasses, herbs, and low-growing shrubs.

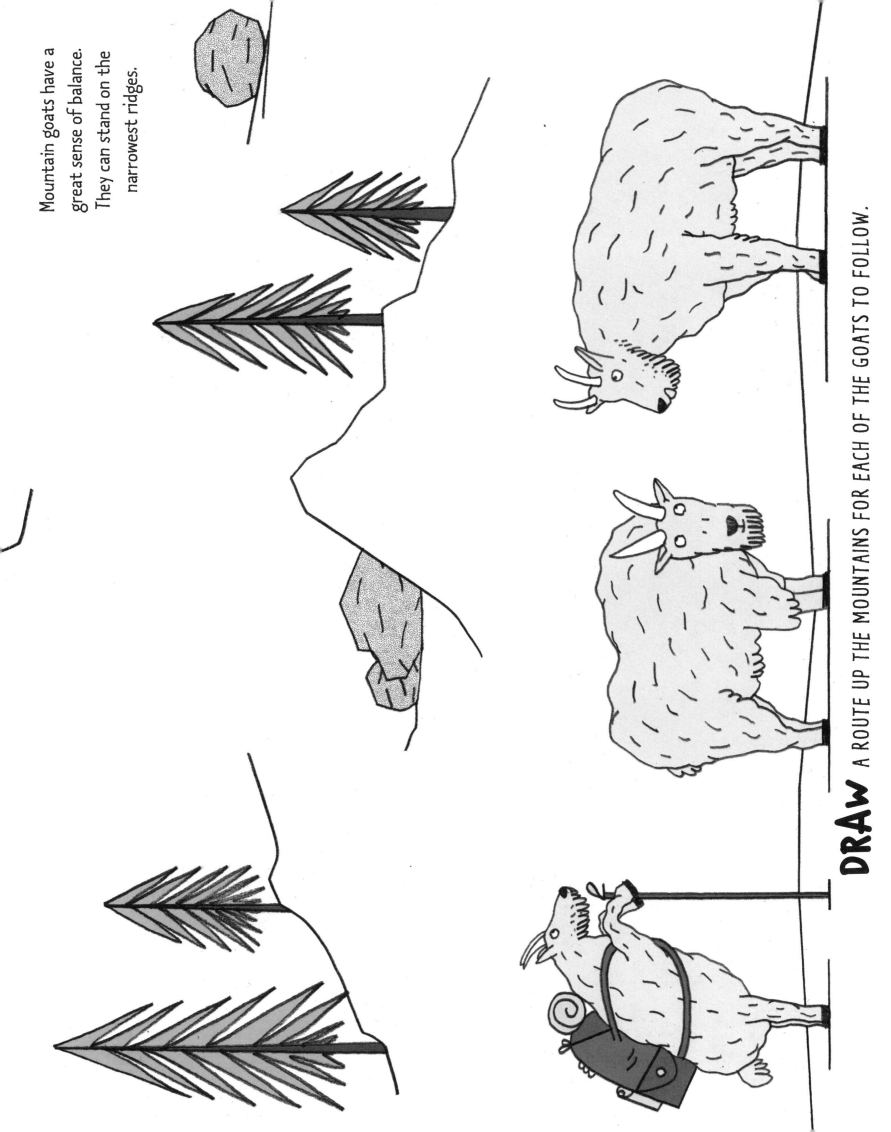

Mountain goats have a great sense of balance. They can stand on the narrowest ridges.

DRAW A ROUTE UP THE MOUNTAINS FOR EACH OF THE GOATS TO FOLLOW.

kitten games

Kittens love to play – with their brothers and sisters and their toys. Playing is fun and it really improves their hunting skills. If you tie a toy to piece of string and dangle it in front of your kitten, it will stalk and pounce on the "prey". These kittens are hunting balls of yarn.

CONNECT THE KITTENS TO THEIR PALS.

At 30 days old, kittens can walk, mew, and play.

Kittens are born with their eyes and ears closed.

Cheeky puffer fish

Going about its own business, a puffer fish looks very ordinary. This makes it seem like easy prey for many bigger fish. But the puffer fish has a trick up its sleeve. It can quickly fill its body with water and turn into a spiky ball that's almost impossible to eat.

Even if a predator manages to swallow a puffer fish, it could be in for a nasty surprise as some are very poisonous.

DRAW MORE PUFFER FISH PUFFING UP.

Puffer fish will only puff
up if they're threatened!

Some people like to eat puffer fish. A skilled chef prepares the fish so that all the poison is cut away.

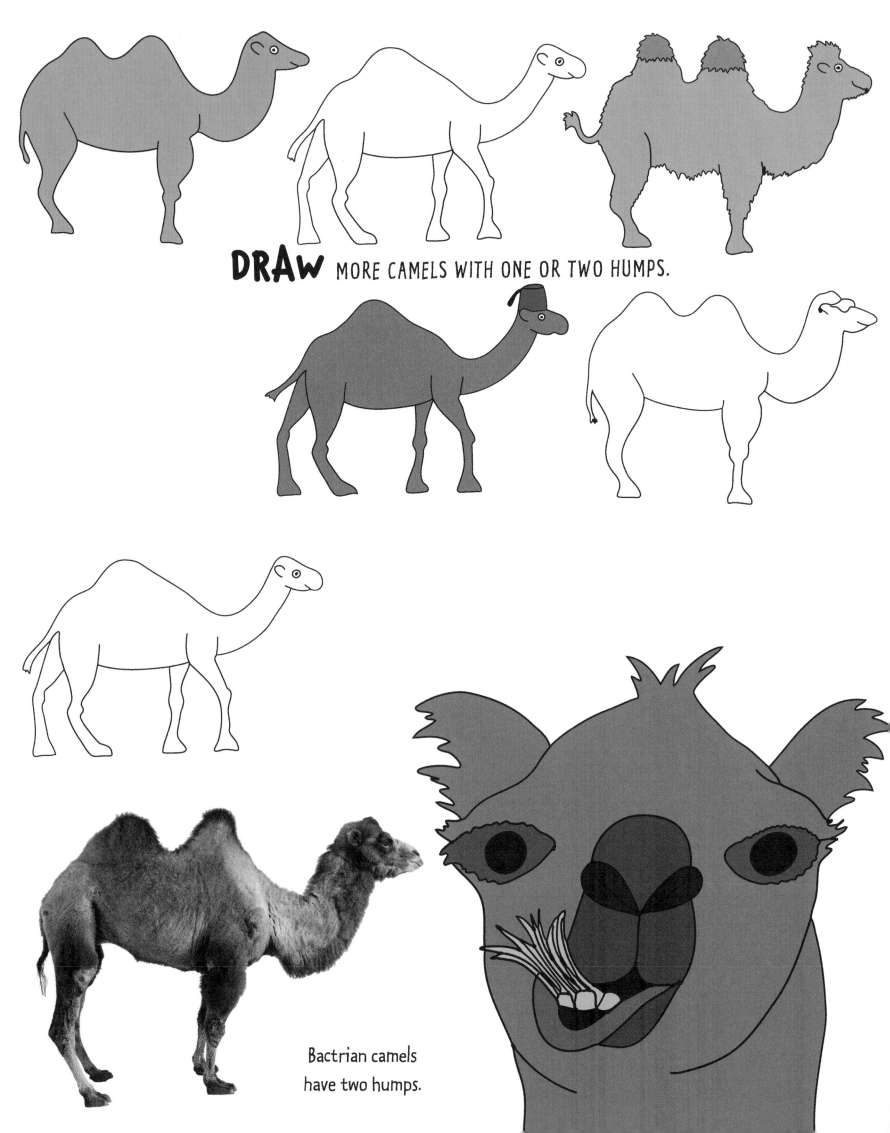

DRAW MORE CAMELS WITH ONE OR TWO HUMPS.

Bactrian camels have two humps.

One hump or two?

Camels live in the desert, and they can go for days without drinking. People once thought it was because they store water in their humps! This isn't true – the humps are actually filled with fat. But the humps do help camels on long treks because the fat inside them provides the camels with lots of energy.

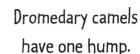
Dromedary camels have one hump.

High in the Sky!

The sky is full of living creatures. Many birds fly, and some travel long distances from country to country every year. Insects such as butterflies and some beetles fly. In fact, there are billions of insects in the air at any one time. Bats fly. They are the only furry animals that do!

wolf-cub club

When wolf cubs are born, they join a pack of about six or seven other wolves, made up of their own family and a few others. The leader of the pack is always their dad. The other positions in the pack are worked out through fights. Wolf cubs practise fighting by playing and wrestling with the other cubs .

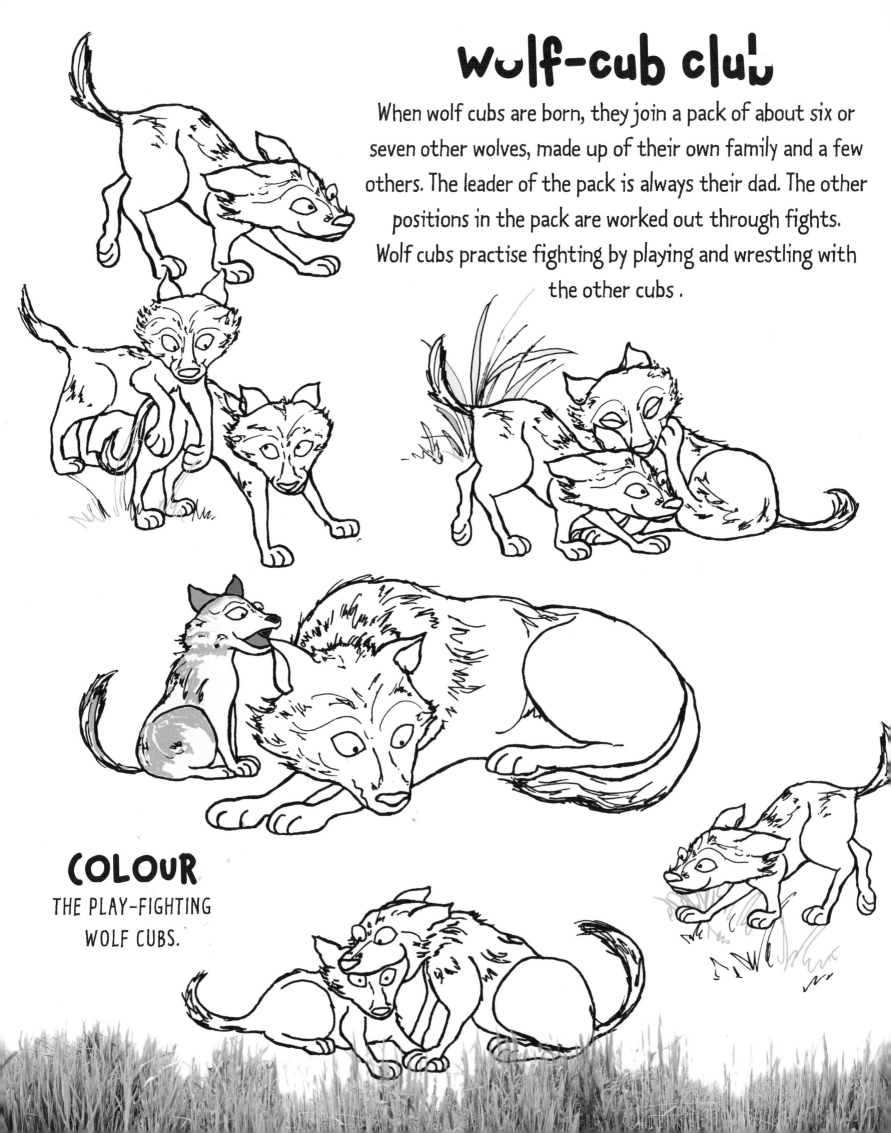

COLOUR
THE PLAY-FIGHTING WOLF CUBS.

Wolf cubs stay with their
pack for one to three years
after they are born.

As wolf cubs grow, they start
to eat lumps of meat that
have been softened for them
by other pack members.

Butterflies drink nectar from flowers through a straw-like tube called a proboscis.

Beautiful butterflies

If you see a butterfly flying from flower to flower, it's probably looking for nectar to drink. But the butterfly could also be tasting the leaves – with its feet! Once it finds a tasty one, it will lay its eggs there. It does this make sure that its children have something nice to eat as soon as they hatch.

COLOUR THE SCENE AND **DRAW** MORE BUTTERFLIES DRINKING NECTAR.

Butterfly eggs hatch into caterpillars. Later, the caterpillars turn into butterflies.

DRAW MORE SQUIRRELS GLIDING BETWEEN THE TREES.

In the air, flying squirrels steer themselves by moving their arms, legs, and tail.

High flying squirrels

Is it a bird? Is it a bat? No, it's a flying squirrel! In fact, flying squirrels don't actually fly, but glide. The skin on either side of their body extends from their wrists to their ankles, making a sheet that acts like a parachute. When a squirrel wants to glide down from a tree, it stretches its arms and legs out wide and jumps.

Flying squirrels are expert pilots. They always land safely – even on narrow branches.

Totally cuckoo

Cunning cuckoos trick other birds into raising their young. They lay their eggs in the nests of other birds. They can colour their egg to match those already in the nest so it is harder for the parent bird to notice it.

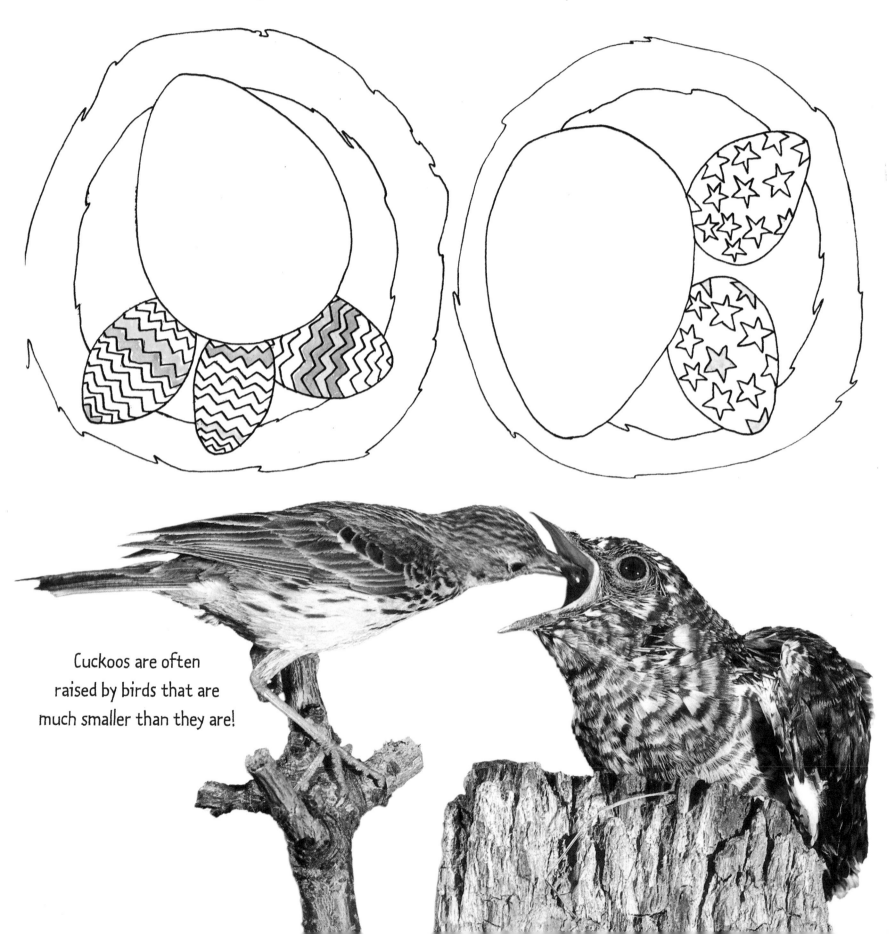

Cuckoos are often raised by birds that are much smaller than they are!

The cuckoo egg is usually much bigger than the eggs already in the nest.

COLOUR THE CUCKOO EGG TO MATCH THE EGGS IN THE NEST.

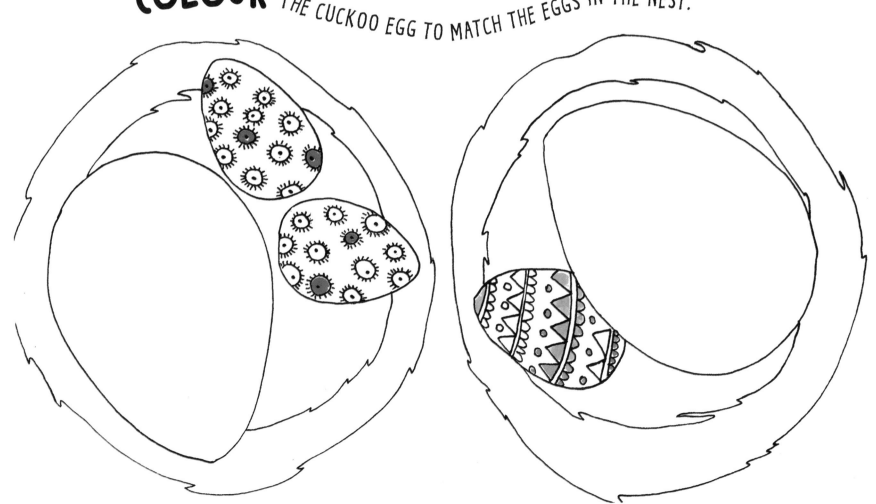

Mole maze

It's a wonder moles don't get lost in their underground tunnels! Their eyes are small – and it's dark under ground – so they can't see very well at all. They also can't hear very much. But their snout is long and very sensitive so they find their way around using their sense of touch.

Moles spend their time under ground eating, sleeping, and digging.

HELP THE MOLES FIND THEIR WAY HOME.

Moles eat worms, insects, and grubs that they find in the tunnels.

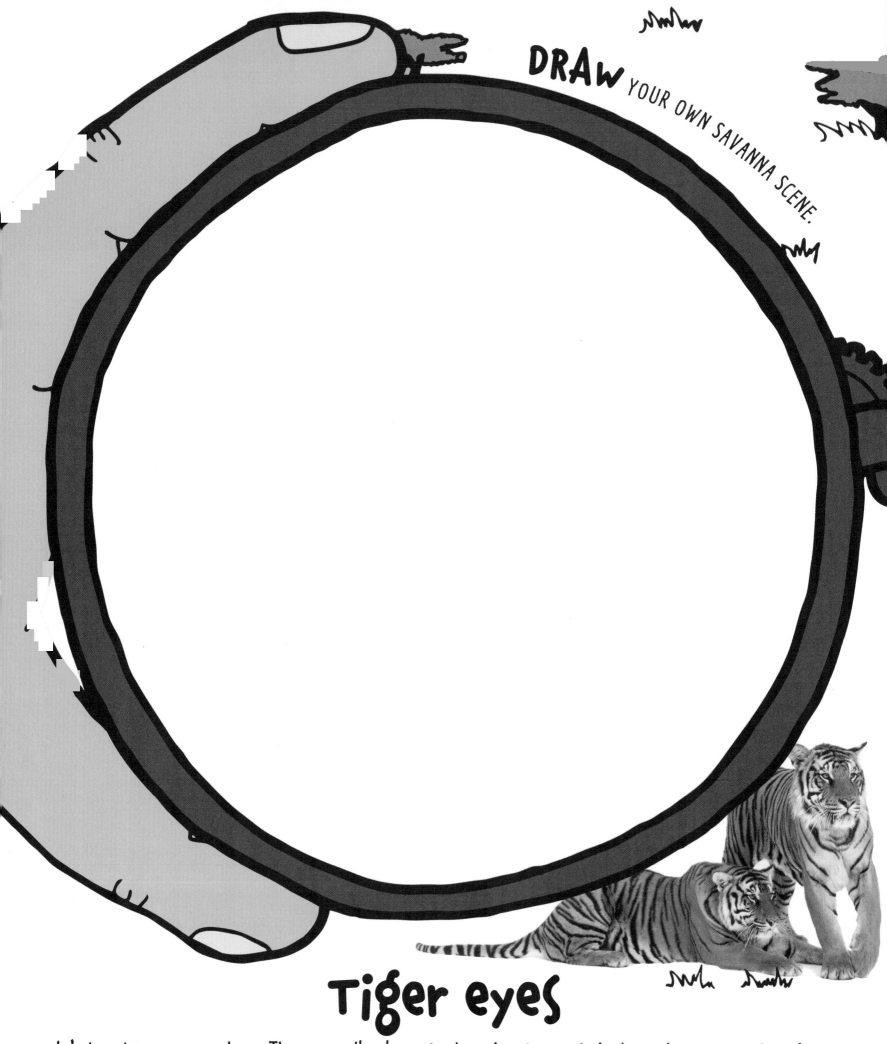

DRAW YOUR OWN SAVANNA SCENE.

tiger eyes

It's hard to spot a tiger. They usually sleep during the day and their stripy coat helps them hide in woodland and grassy savanna. Their black stripes look like shadows in a sunny landscape.

Tigers are fierce hunters.
They eat small animals like frogs
as well as big ones like antelopes.

Tigers live alone, except for
cubs, who live with their
mother until they are about
one or two years old.

Kangaroo kicks

Kangaroos move around by jumping, using their powerful back legs to travel in big leaps over long distances. Their legs are so strong that the biggest kangaroos can jump up to 12m (39ft) in one bounce. That's farther than the length of two cars!

If a kangaroo could kick a rugby ball, it would probably be the best player on the team!

Kangaroo babies are called joeys. They spend the first months of their life warm and snug in their mother's pouch.

DRAW MORE KANGAROOS JUMPING.

DRAW MORE BEAVERS IN AND AROUND THEIR LODGE.

Beavers' front teeth never stop growing! They don't get too long though because they are worn down by the wood and bark the beavers gnaw on.

Beavers eat tree bark. In the winter, they store it in the lake, using the water as a refrigerator to keep the bark fresh.

Beaver builders

Beavers are busy builders. They cut down trees with their strong teeth. Then they use the wood to build dams to create a pool of water. They build their lodge (home) in the pool or on its bank. The lodge has a floor above the water, and it is very warm and snug. The beavers can get to it from the land as well as from the water.

ADD MORE SIX-SIDED CELLS TO THE HONEYCOMB.

Busy bees

Bees do an important job – they spread pollen from flower to flower while collecting nectar to take back to their hives. There worker bees turn the nectar into honey. The beehive is a perfect honey store. It's packed with layers of honeycomb made up of thousands of six-sided cells (boxes) for the bees to fill.

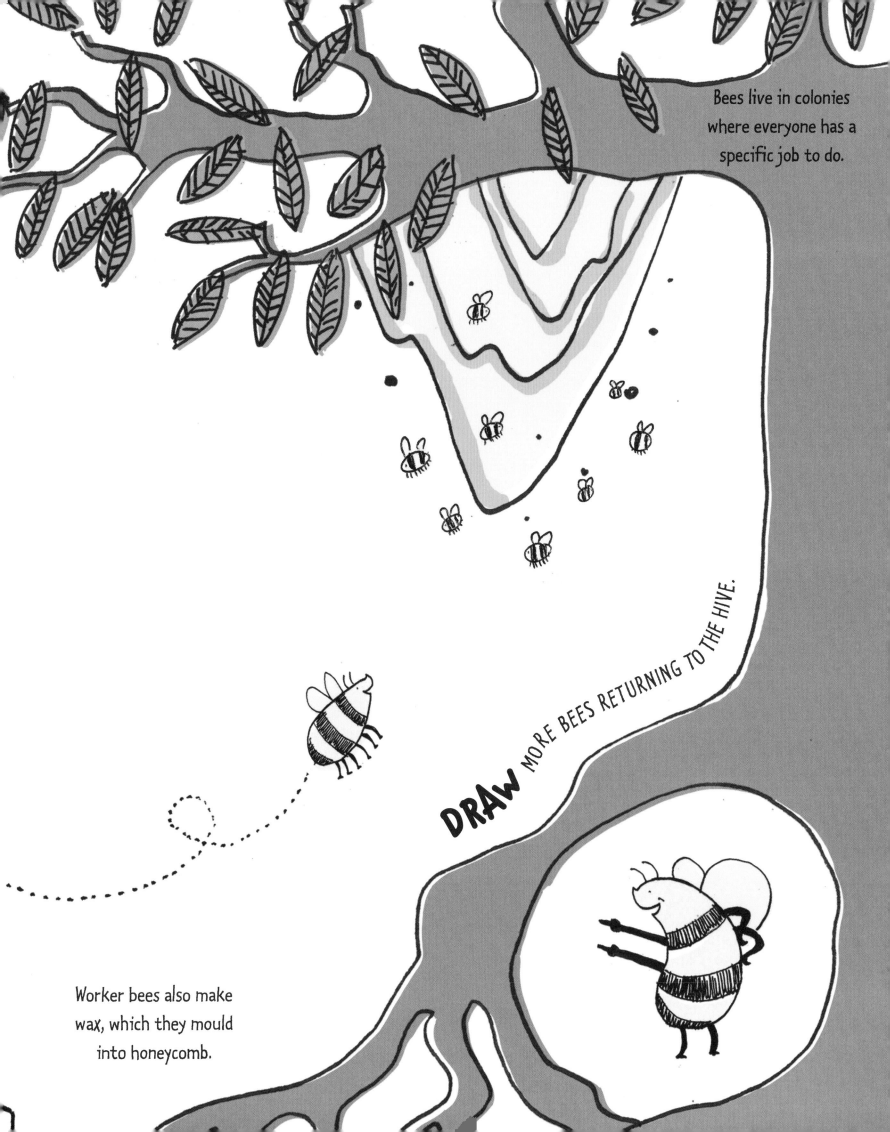

Bees live in colonies where everyone has a specific job to do.

DRAW MORE BEES RETURNING TO THE HIVE.

Worker bees also make wax, which they mould into honeycomb.

Gorillas live in family groups of around 10–15 adults and young.

CONNECT THE YOUNG GORILLAS TO THE ADULTS.

Gorilla campsite

Gorillas spend their days travelling through the rainforest. Every night they build new nests to sleep in. Young gorillas and lighter females sleep in trees while heavier gorillas sleep on the ground.

Gorillas may look scary, but they are actually peaceful plant-eaters.

under the Sea!

The world's oceans are huge! From giant whales to tiny creatures, millions of animals call the sea their home. The oceans are so big and deep that no one knows exactly how many sea creatures there are. There could be hundreds of animals that haven't yet been discovered hiding in the depths!

COLOUR IN ALL THE SEA CREATURES.

Crocodile care

Crocodiles are fierce hunters that catch prey in their powerful jaws. You might be surprised to learn that crocodile mums carry their new babies there too! But when they do, they're very gentle and never close their mouth. The babies are very safe between those sharp teeth.

Crocodile babies hatch out of their eggs on land, but mum soon carries them to the water.

Young crocodiles stay with their mother until they are a few weeks old.

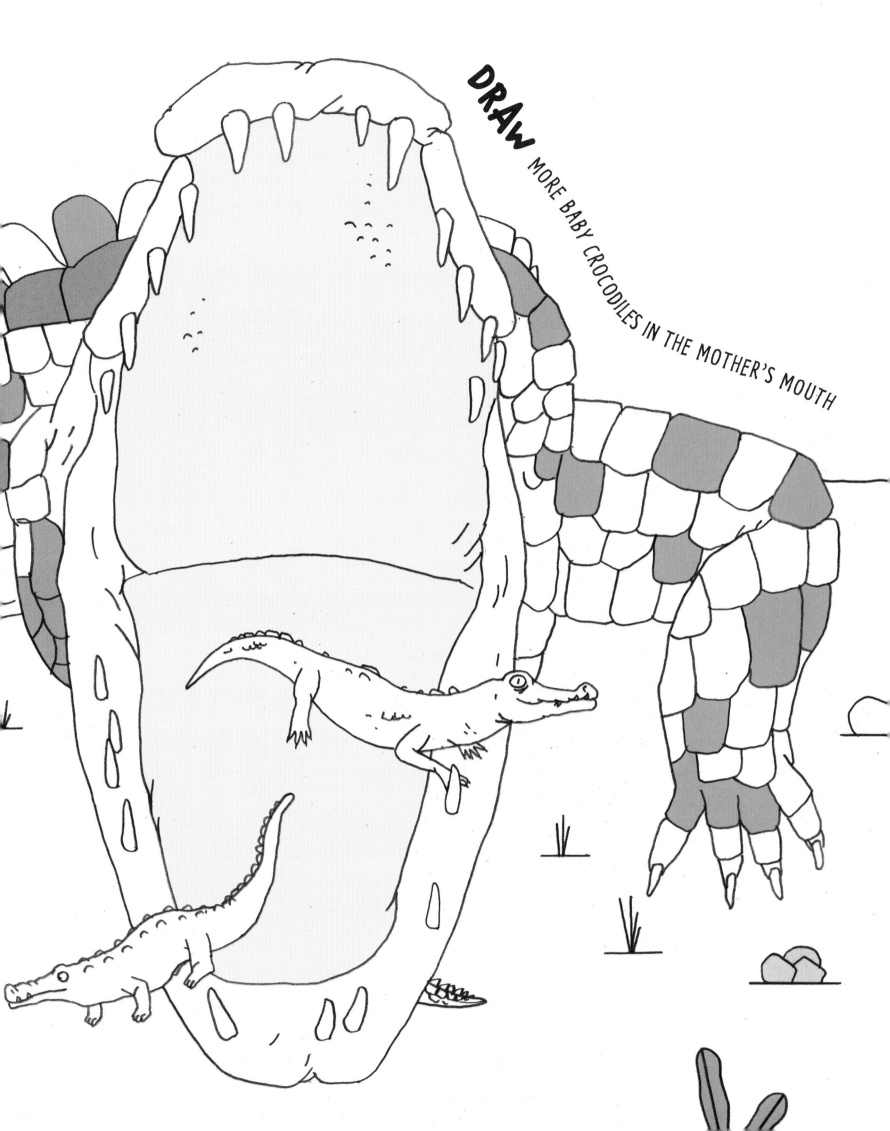

DRAW MORE BABY CROCODILES IN THE MOTHER'S MOUTH

Leap frog!

Ribbit! Frogs are excellent jumpers. They use their powerful back legs to push off, and can jump as far as 40 times their own length. That would be like an adult jumping the length of 6 buses!

Frogs can change direction quickly between hops. This keeps their enemies on their toes!

DRAW MORE FROGS LEAPING BETWEEN THE LILYPADS.

Frogs are amphibians. This means that they can live both on land and in water.

Ear Signals

Horses can't tell you how they're feeling. But they can show you, if you just look at their ears. When horses are happy and alert, their ears stand straight up. When they're relaxed, their ears are floppy. And when they're feeling angry or grumpy, their ears lie straight back in warning. That's when it's best to steer clear!

ALERT

DRAW MORE HORSES IN THE STABLES.

ANGRY

Horses are very social animals, and like to live in groups.

DRAW MORE HORSES IN THE FIELD.

Ladybird, ladybird

You might be surprised to learn that ladybirds aren't just red with black spots. They can be many different bright colours, such as orange or yellow. But their bright colouring doesn't just make them look pretty. It also tells birds that they taste horrible. That's why very few birds eat ladybirds.

Ladybirds eat many other insects. This makes them very useful to people, especially on a farm.

DRAW MORE LADYBIRDS AND COLOUR THEM IN.

Ladybirds sleep through the winter, sometimes snoozing in large groups inside tree trunks or outbuildings.

Lazy hippo days

Hippos like to spend their days keeping cool in the water. Their eyes, ears, and nose are all on the top of their head, so they can stay almost completely under water, and still be able to see, hear, and breathe.

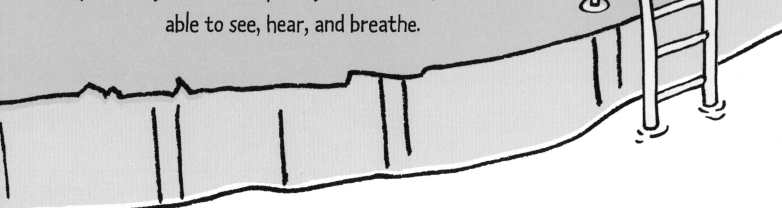

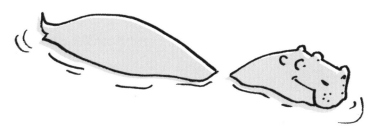

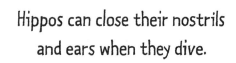

Hippos can close their nostrils and ears when they dive.

Hippos would rather walk along the bottom of a river than swim – unless you give them a rubber ring!

I might have sharp teeth and a huge mouth, but I only eat grass!

DRAW MORE HIPPOS STAYING COOL IN THE WATER.

Pigs in mud

Mmm, there's nothing like a mud bath on a hot day! Pigs splash around in muddy water to keep cool, but mud does another job, too. It sticks to their skin and protects the pigs from the sun's hot rays – a bit like the sunscreen you put on to go the beach!

DRAW MORE PIGS
ROLLING AROUND IN THE MUD.

Being covered in mud also stops the pigs from being bitten by insects. All the more reason to jump right in!

Social Sea otters

Sea otters are social creatures. To stay close to their family and friends, they form floating groups called rafts. Before they go to sleep, sea otters may wrap themselves in a seaweed called kelp. The kelp is attached to the sea floor and keeps the otters from drifting away. Sometimes they even hold each others' paws!

Sea otters float on their back in shallow seas, and they even sleep like this.

DRAW MORE SEA OTTERS FORMING RAFTS.

Sea otters spend most of their life in the water. Their thick fur helps them to stay warm.

In the summer, when the ice melts, polar bears eat whatever they can find. This could be land animals, birds, eggs, and plants – or even rubbish left behind by humans!

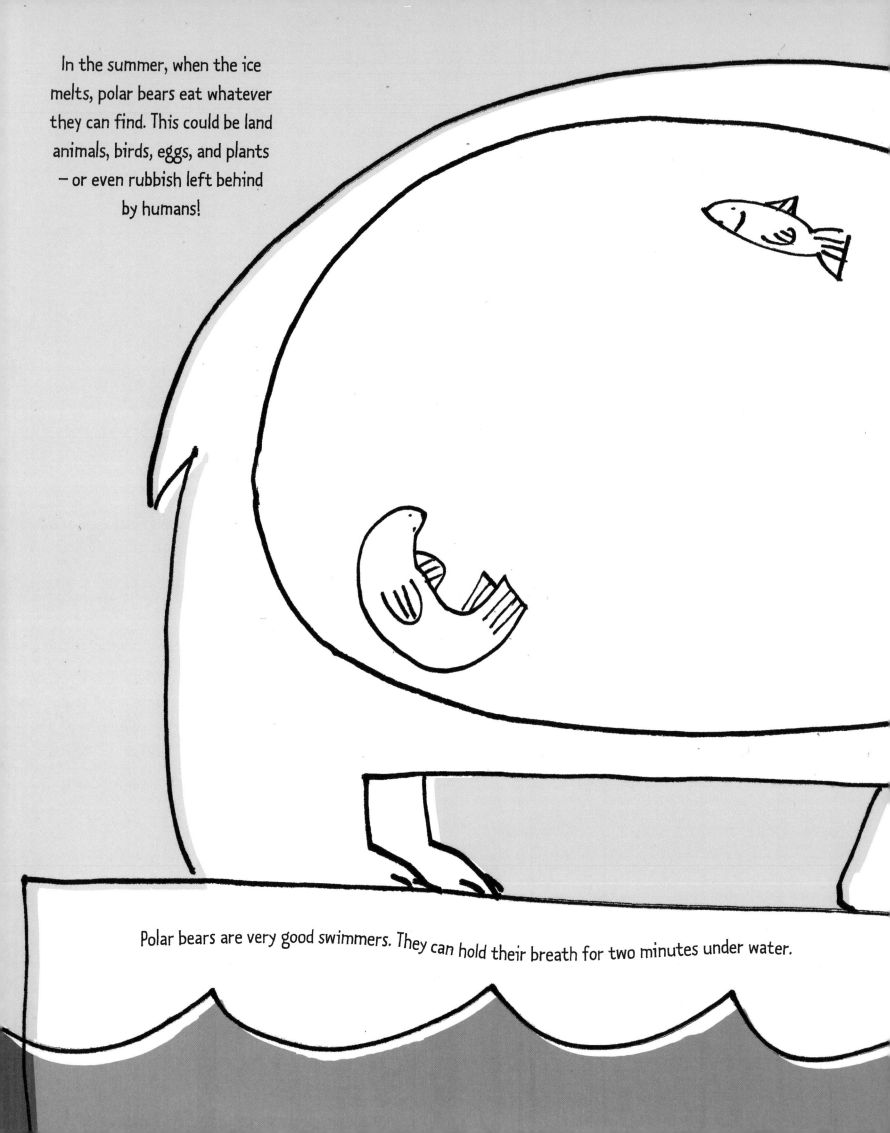

Polar bears are very good swimmers. They can hold their breath for two minutes under water.

DRAW SOME MORE THINGS THAT THIS POLAR BEAR MAY HAVE EATEN FOR HIS DINNER.

Polar-bear hunt

A polar bear may look cuddly, but it is actually a fierce hunter. It hunts seals that also live on the ice. The polar bear's white coat helps it stay hidden when it follows a seal. If the seal turns around, the polar bear stands very still, and the seal can't see it against the white snow. When the polar bear gets close enough, it quickly snaps up its dinner.

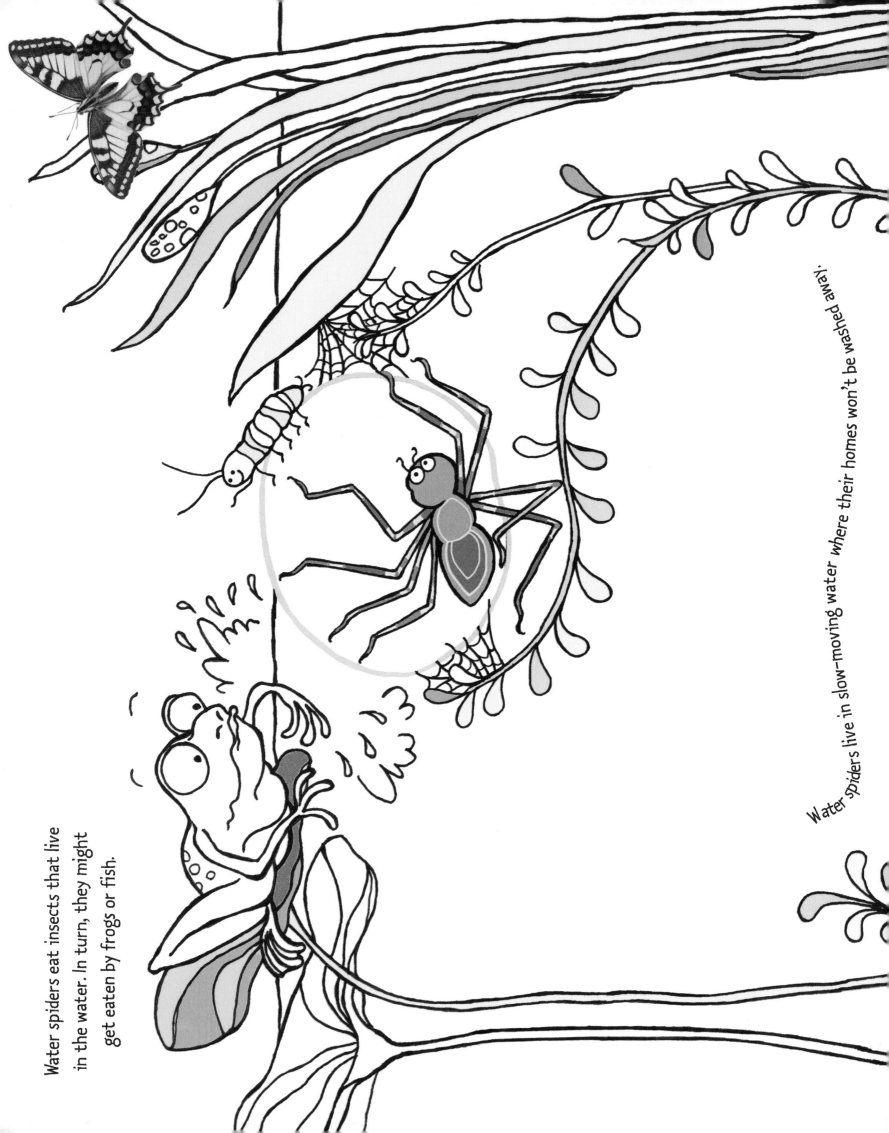

Water spiders eat insects that live in the water. In turn, they might get eaten by frogs or fish.

Water spiders live in slow-moving water where their homes won't be washed away.

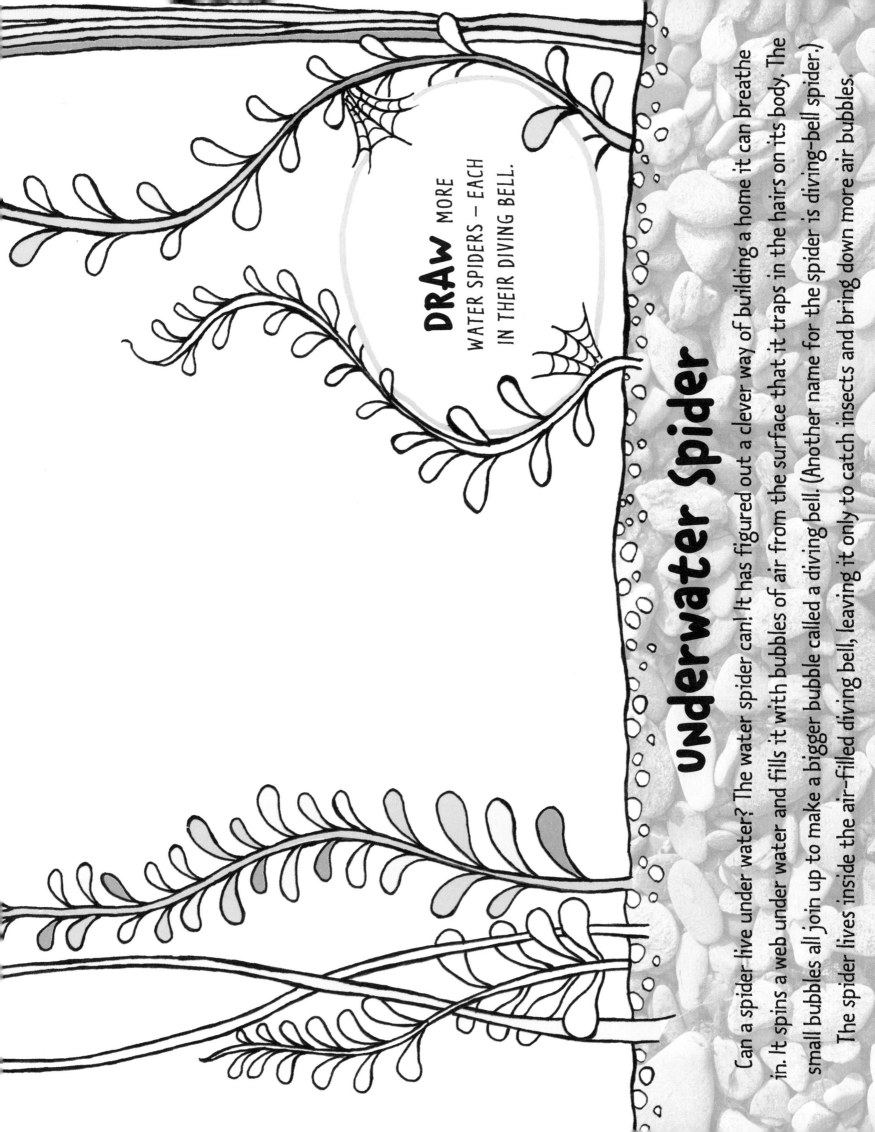

DRAW MORE
WATER SPIDERS – EACH
IN THEIR DIVING BELL.

underwater Spider

Can a spider live under water? The water spider can! It has figured out a clever way of building a home it can breathe in. It spins a web under water and fills it with bubbles of air from the surface that it traps in the hairs on its body. The small bubbles all join up to make a bigger bubble called a diving bell. (Another name for the spider is diving-bell spider.)

The spider lives inside the air-filled diving bell, leaving it only to catch insects and bring down more air bubbles.

When cygnets are small, they're covered in fuzzy grey feathers called down. They don't get their white feathers until they're a bit older.

Swan love

Swans are true romantics. When they meet the swan of their dreams, they stay together for years, and sometimes even for life. Together they make a nest that's more than 1m (3ft) wide. Up to eight fuzzy swan babies (called cygnets) hatch to swan couples each spring. The babies stay with their parents until they are around six months old.

DRAW MORE SWANS WITH THEIR CYGNETS.

Cygnets start swimming soon after they hatch. If they get tired, they may sometimes hitch a ride on mum or dad's back!

whale watch

Whales are some of the biggest animals on the planet. It might surprise you to learn that some whales don't eat big animals, but huge amounts of tiny shrimps called krill. These whales don't have teeth – they filter their food through big hairy plates (called baleen plates) that hang from the roof of their mouth. These act like a sieve, letting only small bits of food through.